HOW TO DRAW CARICATURES

David Antram

BOOK HOUSE

Published in Great Britain in MMXV by
Book House, an imprint of
The Salariya Book Company Ltd
25 Marlborough Place, Brighton BN1 1UB
www.salariya.com

PB ISBN: 978-1-910184-81-3

© The Salariya Book Company Ltd MMXV

All rights reserved. No part of this publication may be reproduced, stored in or introduced into a retrieval system or transmitted in any form, or by any means (electronic, mechanical, photocopying, recording or otherwise) without the written permission of the publisher. Any person who does any unauthorised act in relation to this publication may be liable to criminal prosecution and civil claims for damages.

5 7 9 8 6 4

A CIP catalogue record for this book is available from the British Library.

Printed and bound in China.

Reprinted in MMXX.

This book is sold subject to the conditions that it shall not, by way of trade or otherwise, be lent, resold, hired out, or otherwise circulated without the publisher's prior consent in any form or binding or cover other than that in which it is published and without similar condition being imposed on the subsequent purchaser.

Author: **David Antram** was born in Brighton, England, in 1958. He studied at Eastbourne College of Art and then worked in advertising for fifteen years before becoming a full-time artist. He has illustrated many children's non-fiction books.

Editors: **Rob Walker, Caroline Coleman**

Visit
www.salariya.com
for our online catalogue and
free fun stuff.

WARNING: Fixatives should be used only under adult supervision.

Contents

- 4   Making a start
- 6   Drawing tools
- 8   Materials
- 10   Exaggerating proportions
- 12   Eyes, nose and mouth
- 14   Animal characteristics
- 16   Different treatments
- 18   Insulting vs complimenting
- 20   Gentle mockery
- 22   Macaroni
- 24   Anthropomorphic cars
- 26   Furniture
- 28   Cats and dogs
- 30   Looking like your pet
- 32   Glossary and index

YOU CAN DRAW CARICATURES

Making a start

Learning to draw is about looking and seeing. Keep practising and use a sketchbook to make quick drawings. Start by doodling and experimenting with shapes and patterns. There are many ways to draw and this book shows only some of them. Visit art galleries, look at artists' drawings and see how friends draw, but above all, find your own way.

Use basic shapes and construction lines to make quick sketches that capture the expression and mood you want to portray.

Don't worry about personal characteristics such as hairstyle or eye colour at this stage, just concentrate on creating simple oval head shapes with very basic features to work with.

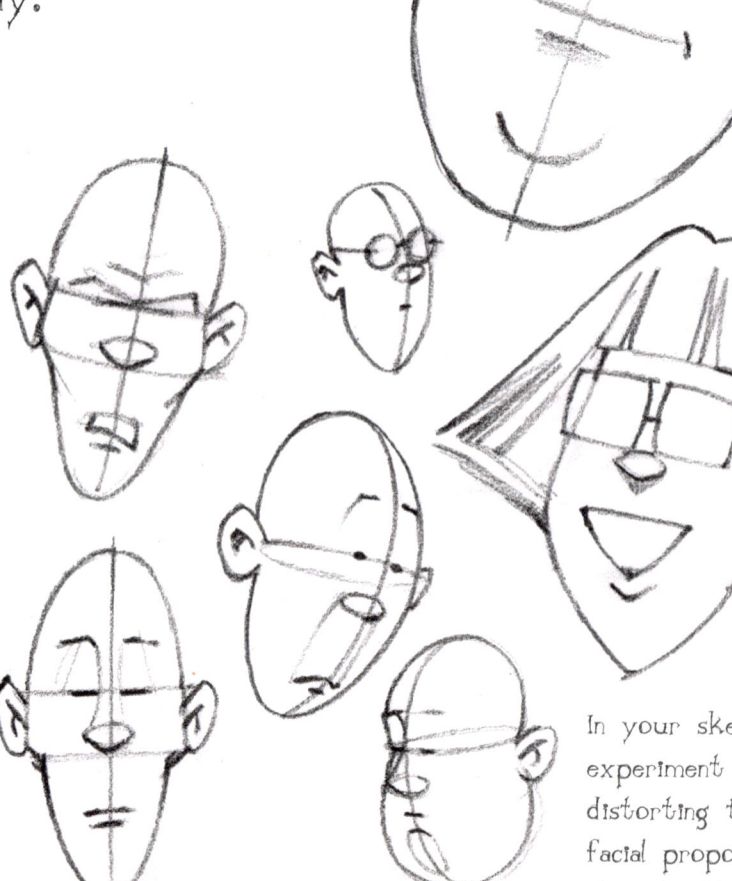

In your sketchbook, experiment by distorting traditional facial proportions — elongate the chin, exaggerate the nose or raise the eye level.

4

Consider the position and angle of your image: do you want your caricature to be looking upwards or facing one side?

Practice makes perfect. If your first attempt doesn't look right, don't be afraid to start again.

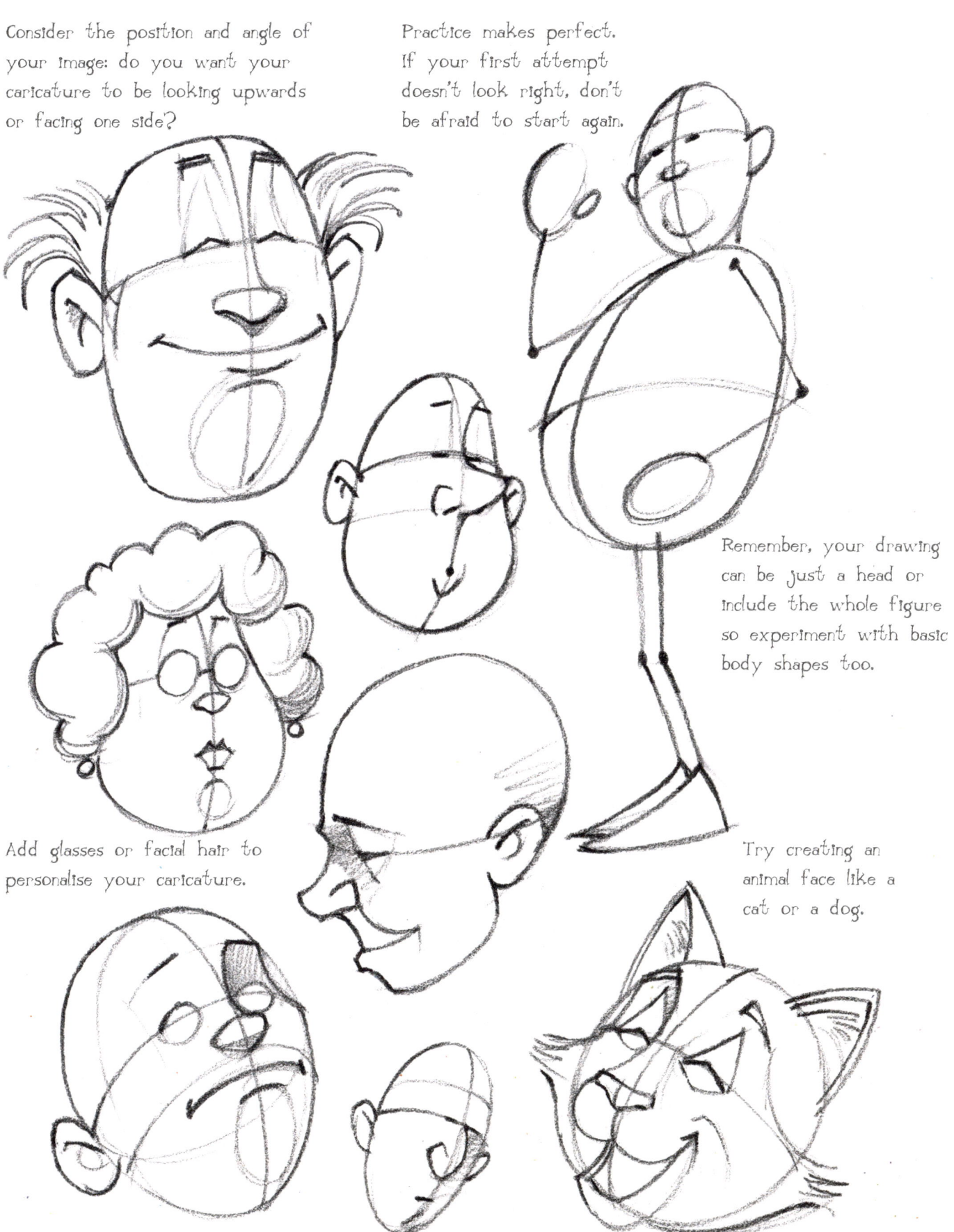

Remember, your drawing can be just a head or include the whole figure so experiment with basic body shapes too.

Add glasses or facial hair to personalise your caricature.

Try creating an animal face like a cat or a dog.

YOU CAN DRAW CARICATURES

Drawing tools

Here are just a few of the many tools that you can use for drawing. Let your imagination go and have fun experimenting with all the different marks you can make.

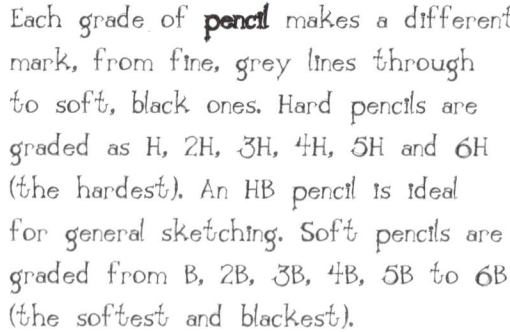

Pencil

Watercolour pencil

Charcoal pencil

Charcoal stick

Pastels

Finger painting

Black, grey and white pastel on grey sugar paper

Each grade of **pencil** makes a different mark, from fine, grey lines through to soft, black ones. Hard pencils are graded as H, 2H, 3H, 4H, 5H and 6H (the hardest). An HB pencil is ideal for general sketching. Soft pencils are graded from B, 2B, 3B, 4B, 5B to 6B (the softest and blackest).

Watercolour pencils come in many different colours and make a line similar to an HB pencil. But paint over your finished drawing with clean water, and the lines will soften and run.

It is less messy and easier to achieve a fine line with a **charcoal pencil** than a stick of charcoal. Create soft tones by smudging lines with your finger. **Ask an adult** to spray the drawing with fixative to prevent further smudging.

Pastels are brittle sticks of powdered colour. They blend and smudge easily and are ideal for quick sketches. Pastel drawings work well on textured, coloured paper. **Ask an adult** to spray your finished drawing with fixative.

Experiment with **finger painting**. Your fingerprints make exciting patterns and textures. Use your fingers to smudge soft pencil, charcoal and pastel lines.

Ballpoint pens are very useful for sketching and making notes. Make different tones by building up layers of shading.

A **mapping pen** has to be dipped into bottled ink to fill the nib. Different nib shapes make different marks. Try putting a diluted ink wash over parts of the finished drawing.

Draughtsmen's pens and specialist **art pens** can produce extremely fine lines and are ideal for creating surface texture. A variety of pen nibs are available which produce different widths of line.

Felt-tip pens are ideal for quick sketches. If the ink is not waterproof, try drawing on wet paper and see what happens.

Broad-nibbed **marker pens** make interesting lines and are good for large, bold sketches. Try using a black pen for the main sketch and a grey one to block in areas of shadow.

Paintbrushes are shaped differently to make different marks. Japanese brushes are soft and produce beautiful flowing lines. Large sable brushes are good for painting washes over a line drawing. Fine brushes are good for drawing delicate lines.

YOU CAN DRAW CARICATURES

Materials

Ink silhouette of Benjamin Disraeli, Victorian Prime Minister from 1874 to 1880.

Ink silhouette

Try using different types of drawing papers and materials. Experiment with charcoal, wax crayons and pastels. All pens, from felt-tips to ballpoints, will make interesting marks. Try drawing with pen and ink on wet paper.

Felt-tips come in a range of line widths. The wider pens are good for filling in large areas of flat tone.

Detail from an 1898 political cartoon showing Queen Victoria and Kaiser Wilhelm II carving up the map of China.

8

Pencil drawings can include a vast amount of detail and tone. Try experimenting with different grades of pencil to get a range of light and shade effects in your drawing.

Remember, the best equipment and materials will not necessarily make the best drawing — only practice will!

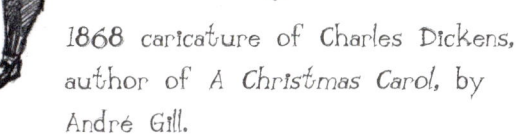

1868 caricature of Charles Dickens, author of *A Christmas Carol*, by André Gill.

Lines drawn in **ink** cannot be erased, so keep your ink drawings sketchy and less rigid. Don't worry about mistakes, as these lines can be lost in the drawing as it develops.

Adding light and shade to a drawing with an ink pen can be tricky. Use solid ink for the very darkest areas and cross-hatching (straight lines criss-crossing each other) for ordinary dark tones. Use hatching (straight lines running parallel to each other) for midtones, and leave the white of the paper for the lightest areas.

Caricature of Charles Darwin, scientist and author of *The Origin of Species*, by André Gill circa 1871.

Exaggerating proportions

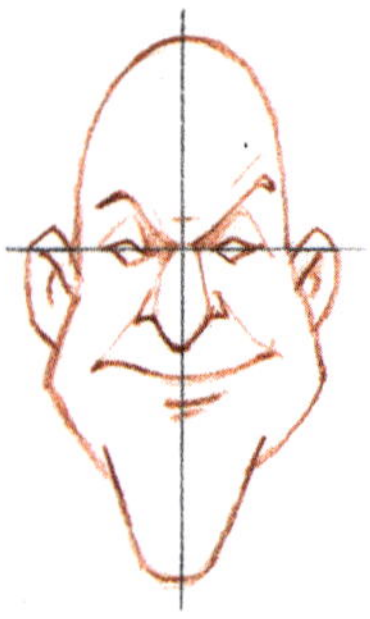

When drawing caricatures, you need to distort and twist the normal characteristics and proportions of a face to exaggerate certain qualities. You could extend the chin, elongate or widen the nose or emphasise bushy eyebrows!

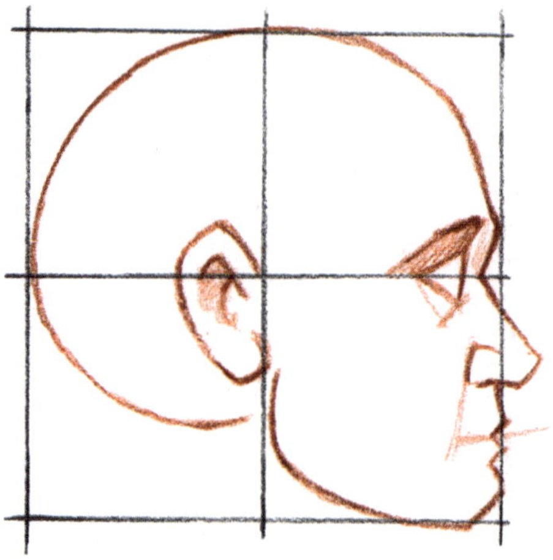

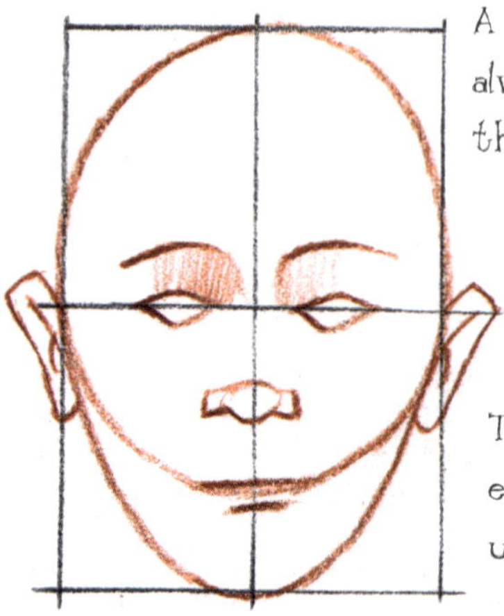

A human skull is always a lot bigger than you might think.

The base of the earlobes roughly lines up with the nostrils.

If you divide a human face into four equal sections, the eyes are always in the middle of the head. The tip of the nose is roughly a third of the way between the eyeline and the chin, and the mouth makes another third.

Begin by drawing a correctly proportioned face. First draw a circle for the head.

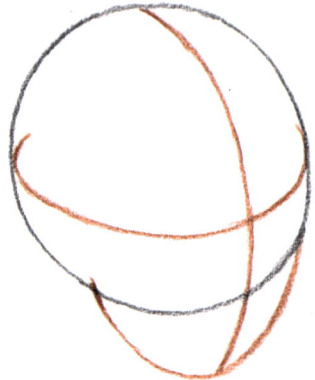
Add construction lines to position the eyes and nose. Add the jawline and mouth.

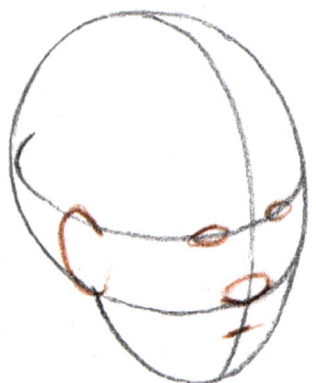
Draw in the eyes, nose and mouth as well as one visible ear. You can erase unwanted lines later.

Use simple lines to complete the drawing details — add a hairline and use shading to create depth.

10

Eyebrows can be incredibly expressive features to define character or mood so experiment with lots of shapes, styles, and positions.

Experiment with the size and proportions of the head. Try extending the jawline or increasing the size of the top of the skull.

Consider the shape of the face — do you want your image to be chubby or gaunt? Decide if you want the nose to be prominent or small.

Try drawing the same image from a side angle. A small difference in facial features can completely transform the look of your caricature.

11

Eyes, nose and mouth

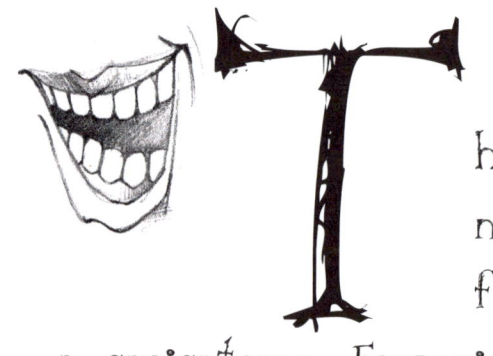

The eyes, nose and mouth are the key facial features for a caricature. Experiment in your sketchbook, drawing them in every shape or form: squished noses, flared nostrils, pursed lips and squinting eyes. Practise achieving maximum expression.

The placement, shape and size of the eyebrows and the extent to which the eyes are open can radically change the emotions expressed.

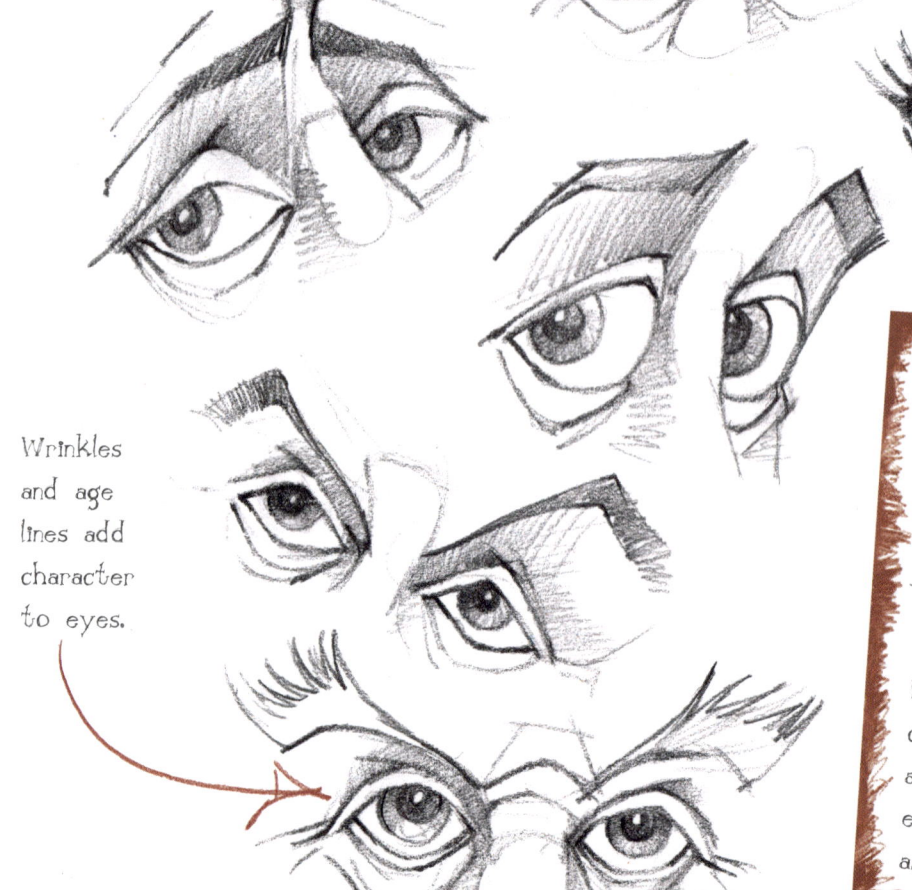

Wrinkles and age lines add character to eyes.

Using a mirror
Be your own model! Pull comic faces in the mirror and sketch them. Your expressions can be as wild as you like.

12

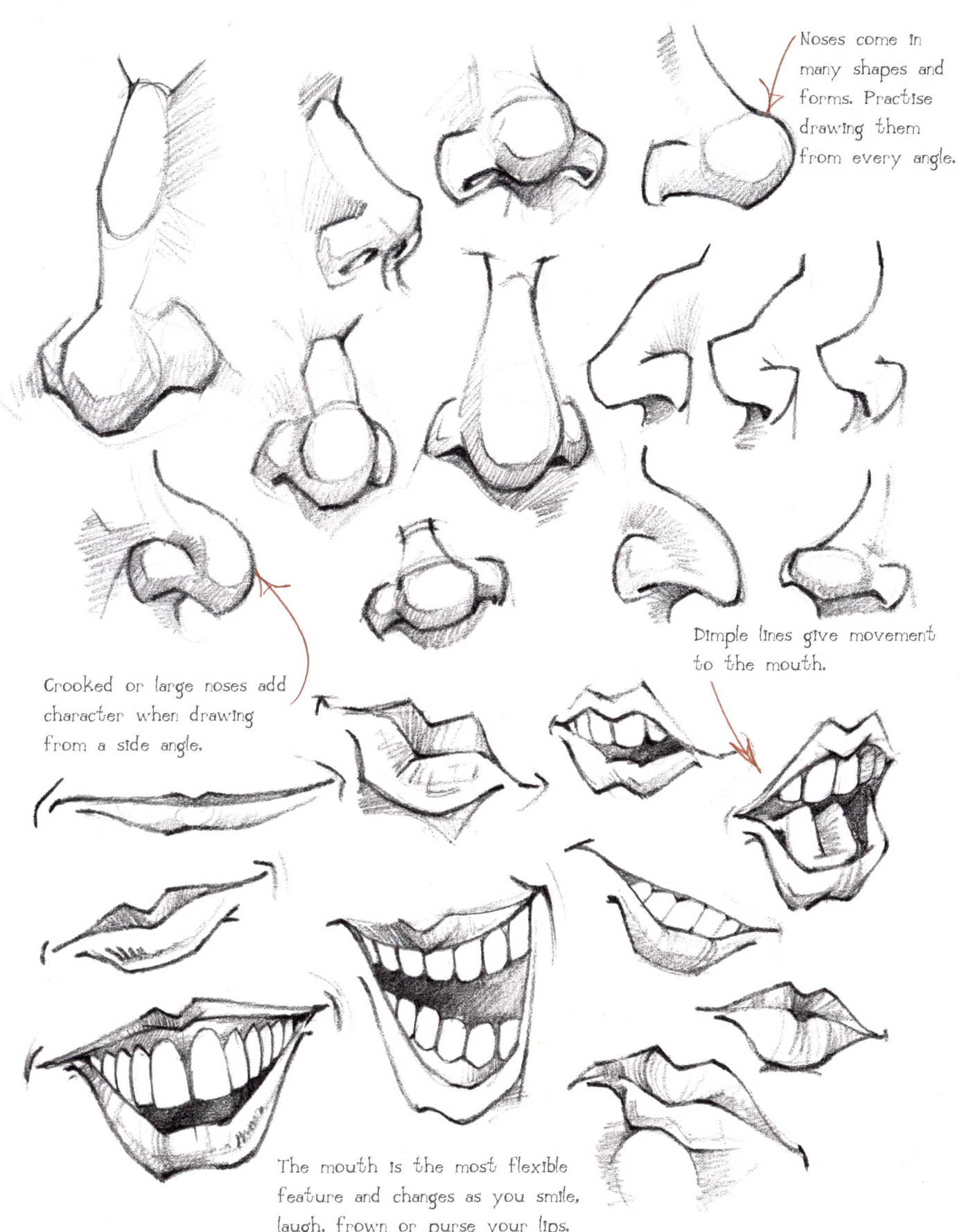

YOU CAN DRAW CARICATURES

Animal characteristics

Introducing animalistic qualities into a human caricature is fun and will expand your drawing skills. It can express additional aspects of personality and will exaggerate key facial features.

Adding qualities of a bird can make your caricature look wise or inquisitive. You must remember to elongate the nose to give an impression of a beak.

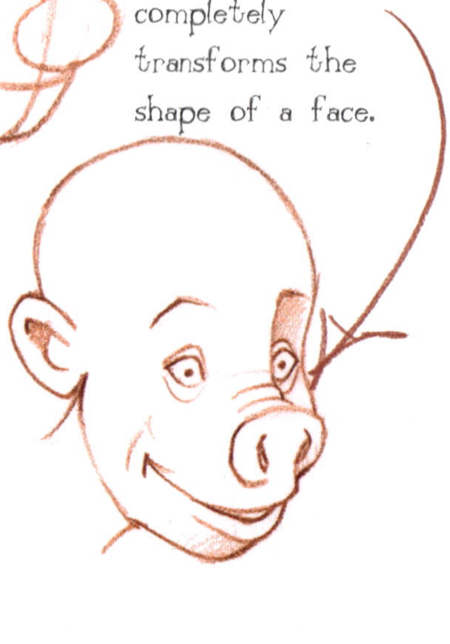

Transforming a face with cat features can create a fantastic feline image. Note the placement of the ears (much higher than in humans) and the change in size and shape of the pupils.

A pig's nose completely transforms the shape of a face.

14

Different treatments

Changing one feature can completely transform the way a face looks. The size and shape of a chin will affect how bold the character looks — superheroes often have a large pronounced chin, representing strength and power.

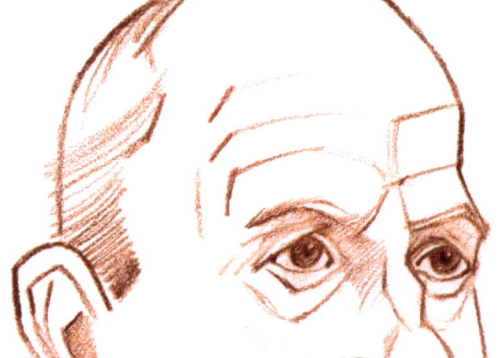

A regularly proportioned face.

Here the forehead has been considerably stretched and wrinkles add extra age to the character.

This caricature has an extended face shape so his nose is long and his chin is prominent, but soft. His forehead is stretched, too.

The curve and size of the chin make this face look grumpy and fed-up.

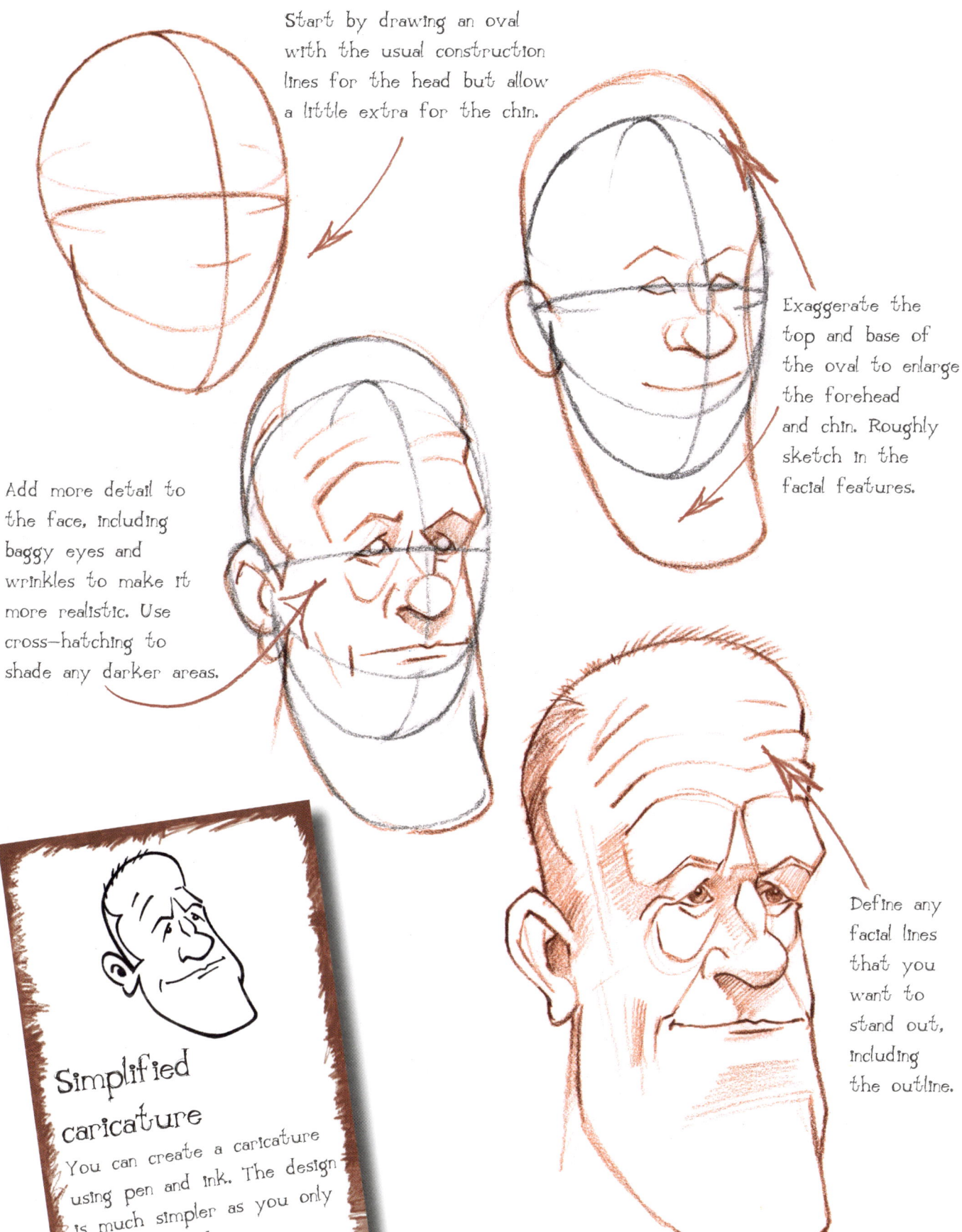

Start by drawing an oval with the usual construction lines for the head but allow a little extra for the chin.

Exaggerate the top and base of the oval to enlarge the forehead and chin. Roughly sketch in the facial features.

Add more detail to the face, including baggy eyes and wrinkles to make it more realistic. Use cross-hatching to shade any darker areas.

Define any facial lines that you want to stand out, including the outline.

Remove any unwanted construction lines.

Simplified caricature

You can create a caricature using pen and ink. The design is much simpler as you only use basic strokes.

YOU CAN DRAW CARICATURES

Insulting vs complimenting

The angles and facial expressions chosen can radically change the look of a caricature to create an insulting or a complimentary expression of character or personality.

Henry VIII was the King of England between the years of 1509 and 1547. He had 6 wives.

Curved features are far less threatening or evil than sharp, pointed outlines.

A wide, dashing smile or sultry pout can show kindness and good humour.

18

YOU CAN DRAW ANYTHING

Start by drawing an egg-shaped oval. Add basic construction lines to position the eyes, nose and mouth.

Add more details to the face including ears and all facial hair. Extend the chin and sketch in the shape of a large, feathered hat.

Finish drawing in the facial features and hat in detail. Make sure the eyebrows are thick and arched, implying anger.

Use hatching or cross-hatching to fill in detail and to add shading. To create a manic look to your caricature, dramatically enlarge one eye and make sure the frown is bold and well-defined.

Remove any unwanted construction lines.

19

YOU CAN DRAW CARICATURES

Gentle mockery

Caricatures do not have to be monstrous or grotesque. The trick is to avoid extending any one feature too much, but slightly emphasise all aspects of the whole face.

Nobel Prize winning scientist, Albert Einstein.

Start by sketching in simple shapes for the head and body.

Large head

Tiny body

Sketch in the arms and legs using straight lines with dots for joints. Add triangular shapes for the feet.

Feet

Start building up all the basic shapes and features. Enlarge the nose and remember to emphasise the lower face to accommodate the distinctive moustache.

20

Use a series of simple lines to define the shape of the nose, eyes, ears and hair. The mouth is hidden by a bushy moustache.

The body is much smaller than the head. Draw in an outfit and some shoes.

Finish off all details. Use hatching and cross-hatching to shade different areas. Emphasise the age lines and wrinkles. Make sure one eyebrow is larger and higher than the other — this gives him an inquisitive look.

Remove any unwanted construction lines.

YOU CAN DRAW CARICATURES

Macaroni

In the mid 18th century, certain well-travelled men would dress in high fashion clothes and wear large powdered wigs. They were known as macaronis and make great subjects for caricature.

Greatly exaggerate the height of the hair. These wigs were so high that the hat on top could only be reached with a sword!

Draw in ovals for the head, hair, body and hips. Indicate the shoulder and hip lines and add a central line for the spine.

Add the arms and legs using straight lines with dots for the joints. Draw in basic shapes for the hands and feet.

Draw in the facial features and hair shape. Make the arms and legs into simple tube shapes.

Sketch in simple shapes for the shoes

22

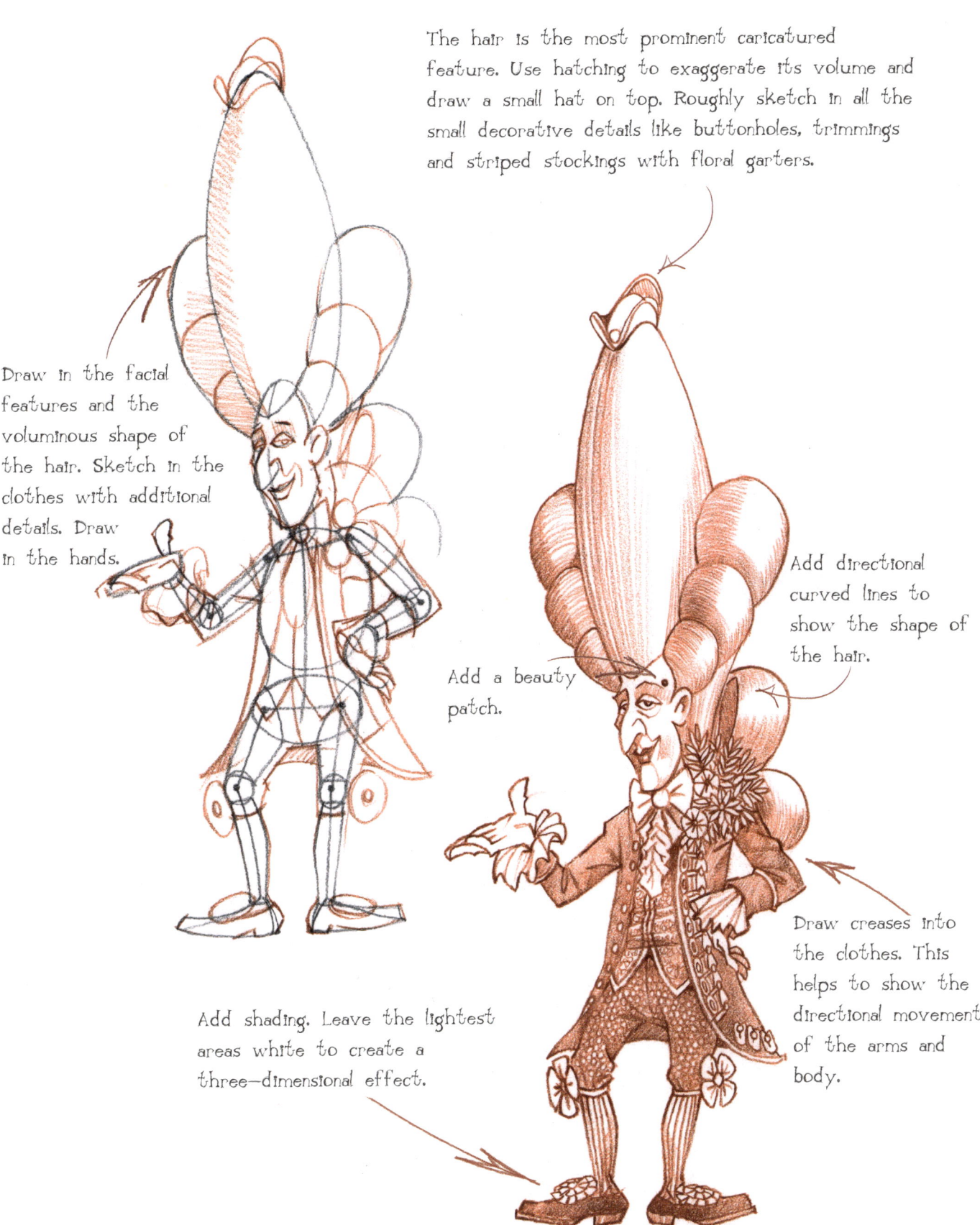

The hair is the most prominent caricatured feature. Use hatching to exaggerate its volume and draw a small hat on top. Roughly sketch in all the small decorative details like buttonholes, trimmings and striped stockings with floral garters.

Draw in the facial features and the voluminous shape of the hair. Sketch in the clothes with additional details. Draw in the hands.

Add directional curved lines to show the shape of the hair.

Add a beauty patch.

Draw creases into the clothes. This helps to show the directional movement of the arms and body.

Add shading. Leave the lightest areas white to create a three-dimensional effect.

Remove any unwanted construction lines.

23

YOU CAN DRAW CARICATURES

Anthropomorphic cars

You can give an inanimate (non-living) object a human personality by replacing some of the parts with facial features — a car's grill plate can easily become a smiling mouth.

Start by drawing the basic shapes of a car — a large rectangle for front and side and circular shapes for the wheels. Don't forget that a third wheel is partially visible from this angle!

Now begin to add some personality — draw in enlarged headlights as eyes and convert the grill into a wide smile.

Draw in the remaining features of the car including windows and add definition to the wheels.

24

Use shading to define the shape of the car and roughly sketch in both anthropomorphic and inanimate detail — draw the eyes, mouth, wing mirrors and grill plate.

Leave some areas untouched. This will make your caricature bolder.

Finish the exterior of the car with block colour, making sure that the tyres are the darkest part.

The light source is coming from the right. Shade in all areas of the car where light does not reach.

Carefully erase any unwanted construction lines.

Furniture

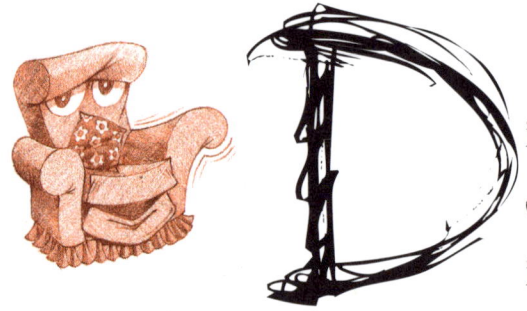

Different types of objects can be turned into anthropomorphic caricatures. You can experiment with the furniture in your own house. Just work out where the facial features should be.

Start by drawing an armchair using simple lines and rectangles to suggest the basic shapes.

Add more detail. Decide where you want to add the eyes and mouth and then apply the corresponding shape and curve to the cushions.

Curve the shape of the arms and the chair top so it looks rounded and comfy.

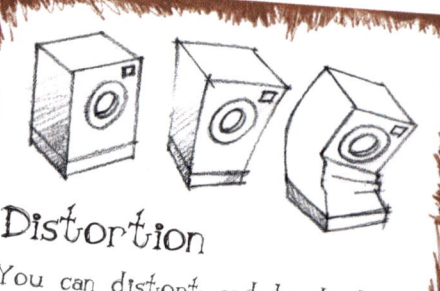

Distortion

You can distort and bend objects to animate rigid shapes.

YOU CAN DRAW ANYTHING

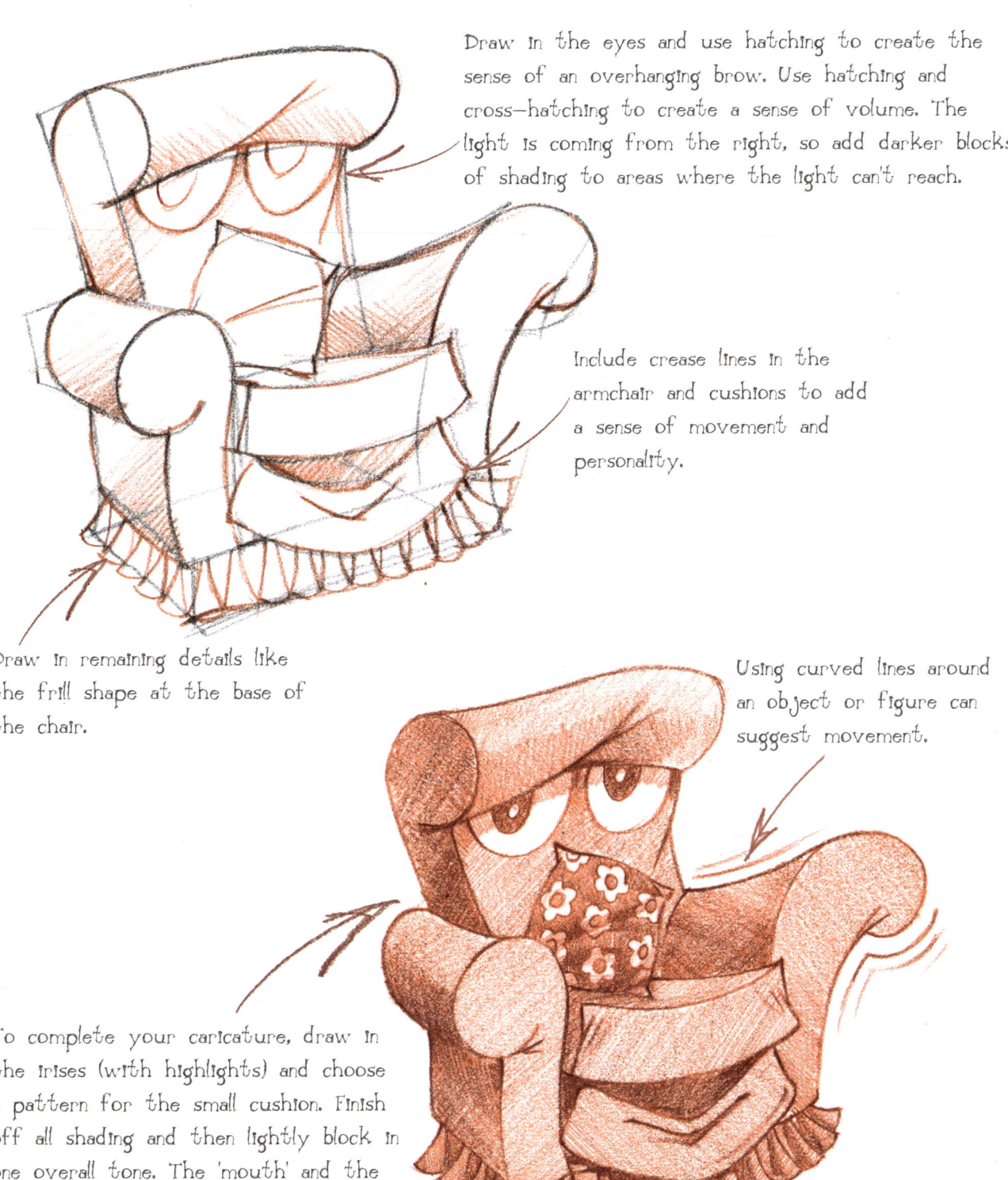

Draw in the eyes and use hatching to create the sense of an overhanging brow. Use hatching and cross-hatching to create a sense of volume. The light is coming from the right, so add darker blocks of shading to areas where the light can't reach.

Include crease lines in the armchair and cushions to add a sense of movement and personality.

Draw in remaining details like the frill shape at the base of the chair.

Using curved lines around an object or figure can suggest movement.

To complete your caricature, draw in the irises (with highlights) and choose a pattern for the small cushion. Finish off all shading and then lightly block in one overall tone. The 'mouth' and the irises should be shaded darkest.

Remove any unwanted construction lines.

27

YOU CAN DRAW CARICATURES

Cats and dogs

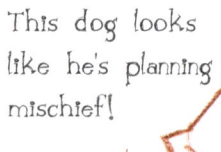

Pet animals such as cats and dogs are good to caricature as you can have great fun expressing their individual personalities.

This dog looks like he's planning mischief!

This dog looks grumpy.

Start by drawing an oval head shape.

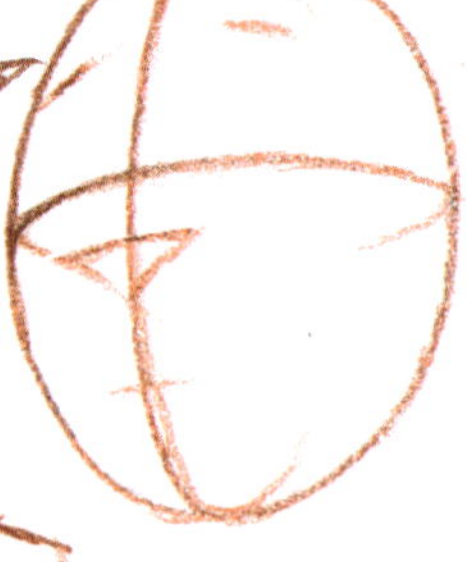

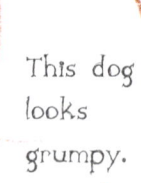

Exaggerate the droop of the jowls to overlap the construction lines.

Ears can be very expressive. Choose if you want them to be upright or floppy.

Eyebrows that slant downwards from the middle will make the dog look sad.

28

Using simple shapes, roughly sketch in the eyes, nose, mouth, ears and chin.

Add more detail to complete the eyes and nose. Draw in the tongue and extend the cheeks beyond the construction lines for added effect.

Always start your drawing with an oval and construction lines – the same as if you were drawing a human.

Finish all details to complete. Use jagged lines for the fur and create added depth with hatching and shading. The eyes are the darkest part.

Remove any unwanted construction lines.

Extreme features
You can push features to extremes and it will still be recognisable as a cat.

YOU CAN DRAW CARICATURES

Looking like your pet

Scientists have found that we deliberately choose pets that look similar to us! Comparing owner and pet can be a fun caricature exercise, particularly if you exaggerate one common feature.

It's easier to choose just one similar feature to distort — large teeth or nose shapes both work very well.

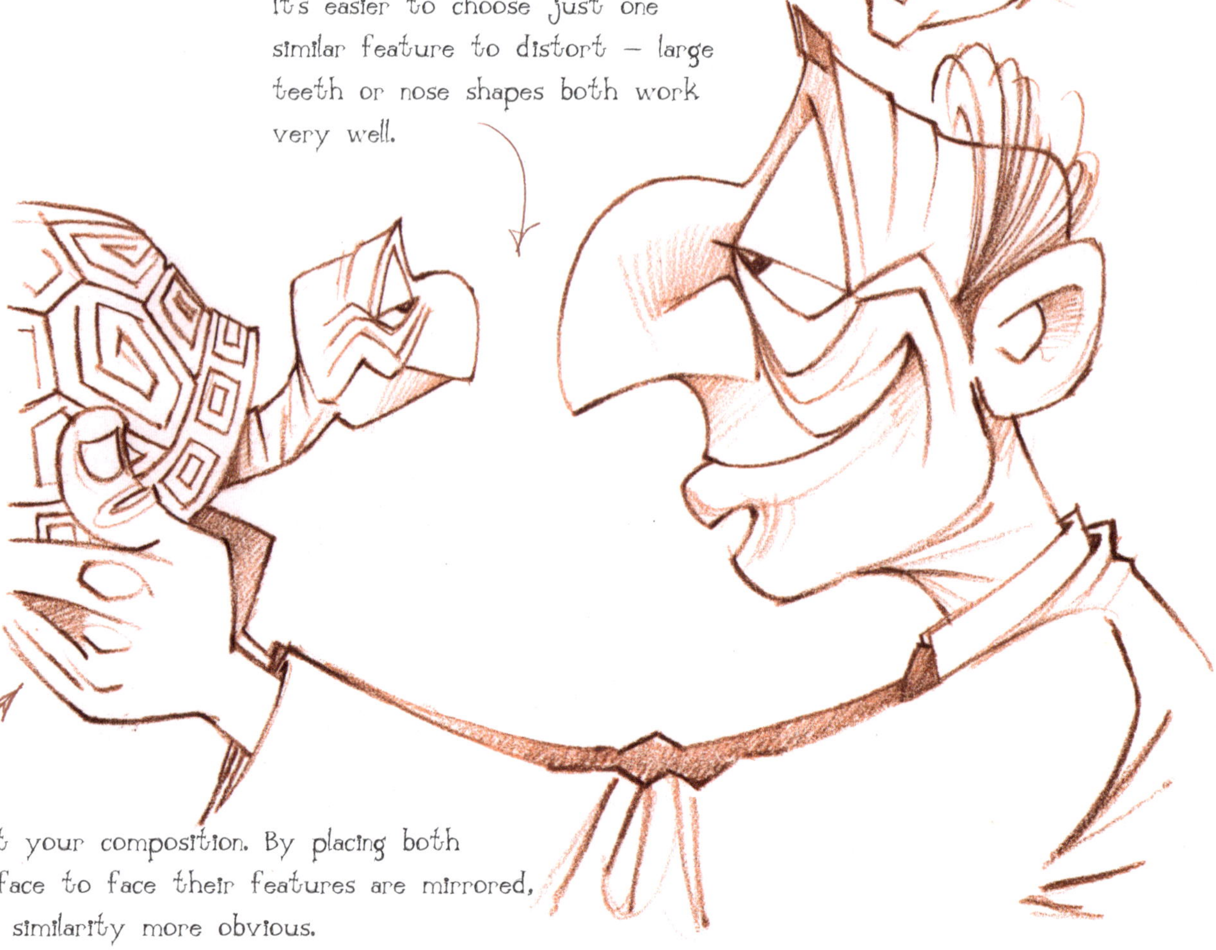

Think about your composition. By placing both characters face to face their features are mirrored, making the similarity more obvious.

30

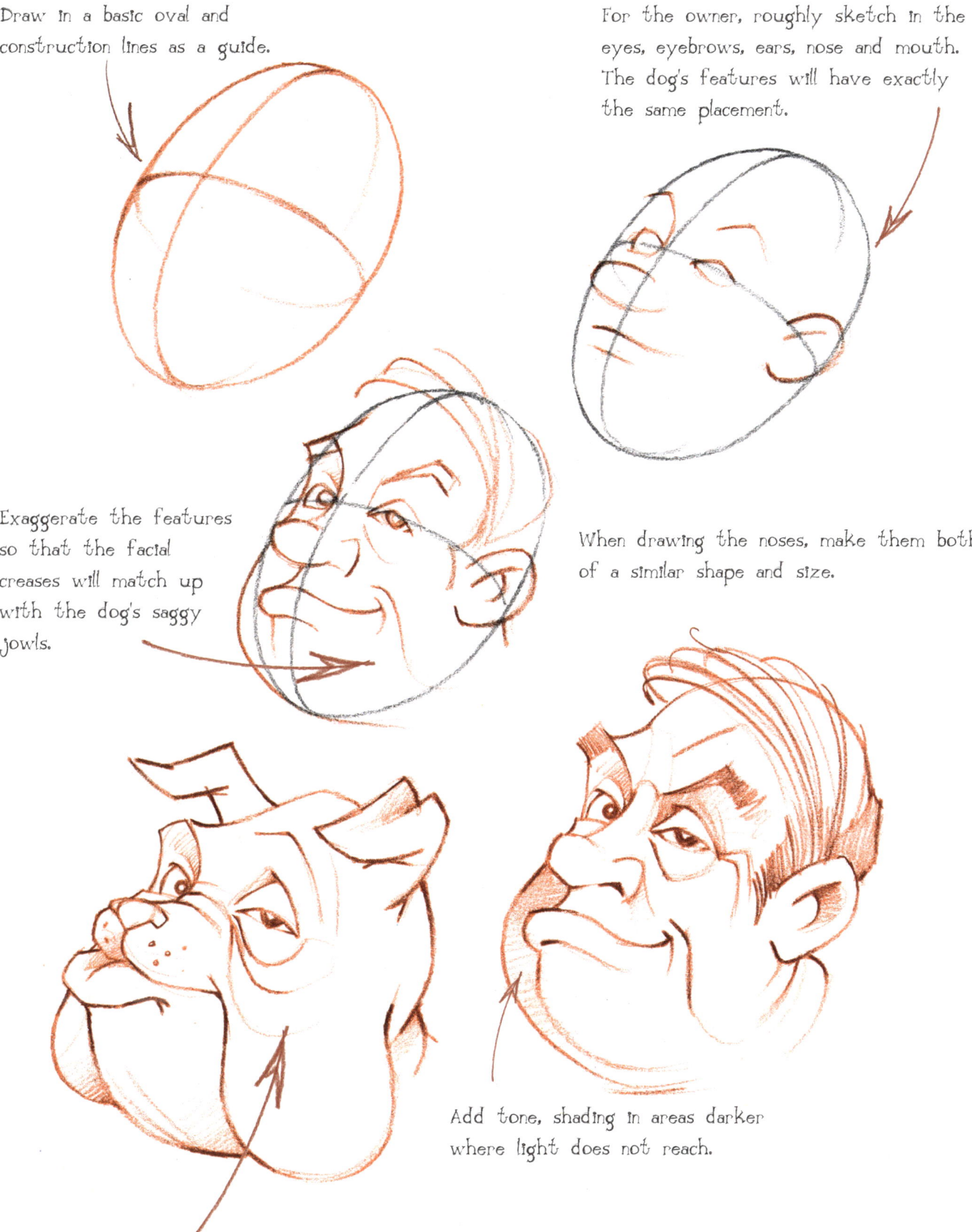

Draw in a basic oval and construction lines as a guide.

For the owner, roughly sketch in the eyes, eyebrows, ears, nose and mouth. The dog's features will have exactly the same placement.

Exaggerate the features so that the facial creases will match up with the dog's saggy jowls.

When drawing the noses, make them both of a similar shape and size.

Add tone, shading in areas darker where light does not reach.

Finish off both caricatures by completing all details.

Remove any unwanted construction lines.

31

Glossary

Anthropomorphism Drawing non-human things or animals as if they were human, or partly human.

Composition The arrangement of the parts of a picture on the drawing paper.

Construction lines Guidelines used in the early stages of a drawing; they may be erased later.

Cross-hatching The use of criss-crossed lines to indicate dense shade in a drawing.

Fixative A type of resin sprayed over a drawing to prevent smudging. **It should only be used by an adult.**

Hatching The use of parallel lines to indicate light shade in a drawing.

Light source The direction from which the light seems to come in a drawing.

Proportion The correct relationship of scale between each part of the drawing.

Silhouette A drawing that shows only a flat dark shape, like a shadow.

Index

A
anthropomorphism 24–27

B
bird 14

C
car 24–25
cat 5, 14, 29
chin 11, 16–17

D
Darwin, Charles 9
Dickens, Charles 9
Disraeli, Benjamin 8
dog 28, 31

E
Einstein, Albert 20–21
eyes 12

F
felt-tip 8
furniture 26–27

G
Gill, Andrew 9

H
hat 18–19, 20–21
Henry VIII, King 18–19

I
ink 9

L
light source 25, 31

M
macaroni 22–23
monkey 9
moustache 18–19, 21
mouth 14

N
nose 11, 13

P
pencil 9
pet 28, 30–31
pig 14
proportion 4

R
rabbit 15, 30

S
silhouette 8
sketchbook 4, 12
superhero 16–17

T
tortoise 30

V
Victoria, Queen 8

W
wig 22–23
Wilhelm II, Kaiser 8